Also by Eugene Babb

Grit and Roses: Stories

poems

by

Eugene M. Babb

Slideshow, Copyright © 2018 Eugene M. Babb

Published in the United States by Third Place Press

All rights reserved. No part of this publication may be reproduced or transmitted in any form or by any means, electronic or mechanical, including photocopy, recording, or any information storage and retrieval system now known or to be invented, without permission in writing of the author, except by reviewer who wishes to quote brief passages in connection with a review written for publication in print and electronic form.

Cover & Book Design: Vladimir Verano

Cover Image Credits:
Front images: 'Sky', 'wet pavement' © Vladimir Verano
'Drum set' ⓒ Beat Buergi, via Flickr
'Bar scene' ⓒ Alan Turkus, via Flickr
Used under Creative Commons License v4.0

ISBN:
print: 978-1-60944-119-7
ebook: 978-1-60944-127-2

THIRD PLACE PRESS
17171 Bothell Way NE
Lake Forest Park, WA 98105

WWW.THIRDPLACEPRESS.COM

PRESS@THIRDPLACEBOOKS.COM

For Cleta Hughes, Richard Dyksterhuis and Chip Hughes.
You are beacons in the storm.

Special Thanks to Vladimir Verano at Third Place Press.

KODACHROME

SLIDESHOW

KODACHROME

Manitoba

Gravel road, sky a gray sheet,
I stop at a log tavern with buzzing neon in the windows.
Pitcher beer, jars of green eggs, sad guitar from a radio.
Cowhands swagger in, boots and belts squeaking, manure on their jeans,
spitting tobacco juice into paper cups.
Little tough guy takes my measure
With a hard look.
 Punches my arm, growls
"I jus' boughta new truck an' I wanna fight!"

Zelda and Ray

Circled by shadows and silver light,
Two dancers elegantly waltz.
Formal, intimate, wedding bands glinting,
Their eyes laughing at mortality.

Turnpike Rest Stop

Midwest midnight, wind-torn clouds,
Icicles crown a bright café.
A solitary traveler
Sits at the counter,
Sipping soup with trembling hands,
His road home a thousand miles long.

Respighi's "Circuses"

Fifty thousand Romans
Perch on rough stone benches,
Jugs of mead and bloodlust,
Under a canopy
Of Spring light.
Martyrs sing
Their Savior's song…
The lions gorge.

Lost Friend

Hands nimble and strong,
He assembles the delicate parts
Of a carburetor,
Laughs as the motor comes to life.
Strums his guitar with joyful elegance,
His beloved cats the audience.
The last time I saw him,
He was rocking on the floor,
Mumbling nursery rhymes
With a sightless stare.

Rafe

A car for a house,
He wrenches the door open,
Tumbles out cursing,
Totters on crutches through the rain.
Returns with a sack, bottles clinking,
Melancholy crumpling his face.

Pioneer Square

Fingerless gloves, gray woolen hat,
Nose reddened by Winter's breath,
He blows a battered horn.
The silence of midnight
A canvas for
His luminous improvisations.

Rehab #1

Twisting in damp sheets,
Hiding from the rough light
Blazing through the window's bars.
Cigarette smoke, crisp nurses,
Scripture written on the walls.
Shaking, weak, I hear Bourbon's siren song and
A woman across the hall screaming.

Coast

Rain sliding sideways through moon beams,
Shore grass whistling, seabirds huddle.
Surf carves the dunes.

Lana

She looks for Elvis
On the jukebox,
Perfume blaring.
Her voice is
Rusted honey, whiskey,
And despair.

Jerry

Master drummer,
Brushwork smooth and cool.
A sonic furnace
Cloaked with calm.

Music

Symphony paints a vivid mural,
Jazz man croons blue smoke.
Calypso's sunny syncopation,
Opera's soaring grace.
Precious sounds,
A soft place to fall.

Memory

Sky a whirlpool of peach and white,
 the skiff planes on a bottle-green bay.
Heading for home,
The sun's arms wrapped around my shoulders.

Dream

Calico wolverines shuffling
Under a liquid moon,
Natalie Wood mixing martinis with
Lobster-claw hands.
What say ye, Jung's disciples?

Drumming

Sketching with
Ancient brass, calfskin and maple.
Soothing rhythms,
Joyous heart.

Bar Girl

Thin, languid,
Lipstick smeared
On a feral grin,
She lounges in a booth,
Her scent sweetly rotten.

Blake's "Red Dragon"

Delicate pastels
Belie the sinister scene.
Lucifer's minion:
Muscles rippling, tail dragging,
A rose-tinted bat-winged beast,
Ravenous for Israel's flesh.

Cranbrook

Winter's white silence,
Cold as a demon's glare.
Spring retreats, howling,
Slashed by the razor wind.

Nightmare

Black fanged terror skulks
Behind the sunset.
Yellow-eyed, voracious,
Feasting on serenity.

Artist

Zoot Sims blows the blues,
Through a rust-bucket horn,
the beauty like diamonds.

Rehab #2

White knuckles, bed sheets are wet sandpaper,
Winged mongrels growl as they fight on the ceiling,
Runny-egg breakfast served by Gargoyles
Wearing starched blue smocks.
Detox is a BITCH!

From a Neighbor's Window

Aria of loss, redemption,
Her voice burns through
The grimy night,
Cauterizing.

Rehab #3

Breakfast through a straw,
Tranquility from a needle.
Angelic white coats hover and
Probe for sanity.

Haiku Tribute

Dim bar, layered smoke,
Soldier hunched over whiskey,
Red eyes dripping pain.

White cold sun rises
Over snow-flecked highland plains,
Wolves howl with delight.

Planes whistling, roaring,
Constant sirens, neighbors screech,
Urban lullaby.

Cymbals sound like rain,
Drums are thunder and lightning.
Sax man braves the storm.

Tendrils of white mist
Entwine the darkened roses,
New day awakens.

Meat Market

Wine addled women preen and bray,
Earrings flashing, perfumes clashing.
Through thick smoke
Music bumps, grinds, teases.
Lotharios with lupine smiles stalk their prey.

Eugene M. Babb lives in Seattle, Washington.

www.ingramcontent.com/pod-product-compliance
Lightning Source LLC
Chambersburg PA
CBHW060543080526
44586CB00012B/844